...This is another unfolding, another breaking through the veils, another conundrum, another mystery unpacked that butterflies away. Got the typescript today & am reading it w/ delight & insight & huge regard for the vagabond purity of your unique work. Nothing like it, nor shd there be...

At last, a full-scale collection of LLL's under-the-radar poetry. An essential gathering of her work. Visionary, musician, translator, L's work is sui generis, true to her keen & keening mind & deep soul flashes. No recent American poet has so consistently been in the light & shadows, so restless yet so centered. Resistant & resilient in her certainties & questions. Diamond flashes of light in the world & beyond it. I've been reading her small books & fascicles & translations for — at last some sense of her work's range is now available.
   David Meltzer, *That BeatThing, Lilith, Selected Works of David Meltzer*

The Book of L speaks to the "hidden reader" embedded in each of us – capable of unflinching honesty, wrenching sadness, and divine love. Imagine a world in which compassion and humility informed our attempts at understanding the often devastating juxtaposition of cultures and realities thrust upon us.
Louise Landes Levi contemplates dream and "the end of/ dream," a changeless state and how it transforms the "I", the listener, the watcher, and the "myriad song." Firmly devotional, and drawing from a vast range of traditions and thinkers, Louise Landes Levi is treasure, a rare nomadic mystic poet of our time.
   Laynie Browne *Daily Sonnets, Rebecca's Letters, Pollen Memory,*
                   Original presence, et. al.

LLL's continuous poem:
a fresh, outrageously untamed voice cries, dances, jumps, sleepwalks ingenuously from the hilarious, the mundane, the eccentric, to the profound, the playfully erudite, even the pious a poetry so natural - it seems to breathe

I see the footprints of the dog/
 then I
   see
    the
     dog,

      l wonder
'Will Wittgenstein / solve my problems'?

      Dorothea Franck, author *ex nihilo nihil*

The Book L

The Book L

Louise Landes Levi

Coolgrove Press

Copyright ©2010 by Louise Landes-Levi

First published and in print in the United States by
Coolgrove Press, an imprint of Cool Grove Publishing, Inc. New York.
512 Argyle Road, Brooklyn, NY 11218
All rights reserved under the International and
Pan-American Copyright Conventions.

www.coolgrove.com

For permissions and other inquiries please visit coolgrove.com

ISBN 13: 9781887276559
ISBN 10: 1887276556

Library of Congress Control Number: 2010935513

Printed and bound in the USA

The poetry is the geography of an island – welcome, to the nature of mind..If I cld. welcome you to the 'essence' of mind, the situation wld. be a lot different.
This book is the first of an informal trilogy.

COLOPHON
Some of these poems
have been printed online
www.otoliths.com, www.unlikelystories.org
www.tinlustermobile.com & in
On The Islands w. Norbu Rinpoche
& *For The Time Being*
& <u>*Heavy Metal Poem*</u>

W. grateful thanks: to the editors of the above publications,
to Esther Lamble & Casa di Esther, my office on
Isla Margarita & to Tej Hazarika who heeded
the suggestion of my grandfather
Nathaniel Hawthorne Levi
(1861-1942)
founder of the Brooklyn Public Library
to publish this & other of my works.

for
NN
& the birds
of Isla Margarita

◆

The title of The Book L is taken fr. Bert Schierbeek's
Dada masterpiece *Het Boek Ik* (The Book I) translated into English
by Charles McGhehan, see *Shapes of The Voice*
Twayne Publisher, Boston 1977
In memoria, Charles

Editor: Marlene Hennessy

Author portrait: Solangi del Vale
Cover Art: Barbara Mohr
Photography: LLL

Coolgrove Press
2010

"What I want then, is lyricism, pure & proper, a purely esoterically determined poem"

Paul van Ostaijen

The Book L

In
my life
what absorbed me
was poetry? IS poetry & the
plants/ fr. there to the proportion of music/ I
was quite involved w. religious instructions
but grew bored w. the endless
gossip among the
disciples/

The plants did not gossip/ nor
the notes/ I was absorbed in the lines
between circumference

&

periphery/

The
day I met you, my soul ceased
to tremble between beginnings & endings/

I found in the quiet of yr. countenance,
the disciplinary trajectory of which I was in need/

You
were, of course, formless, yet I occasionally wld. perceive yr.
form, indeed your precise expression, in
the random faces I encountered
&
sometimes in the kind expressions of distant friends
who knew my longing was to be closer

        On
    one such occasion, after
receiving a vision of your early years I met
you in a café/ it was precisely 5 hours between
    the vision & the meeting. I hid my eyes
    in shame & glory. You must have noticed for
     you soon left, that was the last time
              I
           saw
                 you,

    Other faces peer into mine, yet
                        I
                           still
  sleep, waiting for the dawn vision —
     my frail body & mind offered
        to the realization of
            the
                  visionary
                  quest.

✧

'not that I wanted him to do something unusual to me'

Bagnore Gr. 2006

ONE
DAY, while surveying
your countenance, I came across
an unknown land/ at first afraid to enter
the portals of your periphery/ I finally took courage,
&
found myself in the oscillating warmth of
an ocean I had formerly,
neglected

In
the depths of this ocean, were coral reefs
I had not noticed, fish & many mineral rocks, those minerals
were also in my blood, I found
the perception of your voice deeper than the
depths of this ocean, I followed its vibration & found myself in
a canyon of harmonic
d

      i
       s
      c
   i

  p
   l

  i
   n

  e

I
heard the voices of
my
d
  e
a
d
my dead poets/ vividly
in communion w. this depth &
w.
you,

I
went deeper,
& found the heart of love,
inviolate,

I
went deeper
& found myself on a street
corner in NYC where once we had
met, just at that moment, I
was dancing, &
no ordinary

d

a

n

c

e

When
you called me, I missed the
call/ when you invited me, I refused the invitation
I don't know why,

when we met on that street corner,
it was for eternity/ we wld. not part again
& you & I

both

      k
       n
        e
         w

                IT

Bagnore Gr. 2006

❖

THE WOMAN IN RED

The
woman in red
on the island
    of
        dream
is
  my

MODEL

She fasts for weeks on end,
eats wild berries, rings bells & lives
on the mountain/ annoying
the
    conservative,

formerly large & lonely.
rigid, secretly sad/ now she is slender
&
  often
    laughs

✧

One night
she crept into the guru's house/ who knows what she wanted / she was
'caught' kissing his feet/ thrown out by the guards, tho' still permitted
to hang around she began to

      manifest

      unusual

      powers

Girls: STOP EATING & LEARN TO SING

nb. STOP eating the bullshit you are being fed & celebrate your essence, whatever it is.

Bagnore, GR. July 2006

HM & ME

Everyone
wants to know abt. Michaux/ I already wrote
about him but they want to know more,

All
I remember are the old
men in the café where I did the translation
& the tailor, the quiet man who sold suits/ they're
gone now, the men, the suits, the poet

I
visit the place & smell the
old aromas, I must be dreaming them/
I see things as they were & as they are/

Knowing
I can't explain
to you what it was really like,
what the great man & I really said, as the afternoons wore away,

reading poems & chatting
like any 2
old
friends

Bagnore Gr. 2006

◆

HER PET 'GANESH'
after a gig on Christopher Street

Received many flowers & also food offerings/
I was exhausted. But it was exciting
to be in
ROCK STAR
dominion

✧

A
grey car drives up
& suddenly it's like you're still here
& I'm not some ascetic but fucking you
in
Harlem

✧

Ira
gives a great reading
& I am reminded/ O sweet dominion
of luminous intimacy/ I fan the fires of luminosity & raise the dead,
raise the dead, w. my light

&

good
intention.
It's time to leave the USA/ it's impossible
to *feel* anything here, except late at night when I am w. my music teach-
ers, but
that's
rare

✧

Ira
never asks me where I've been
& what I've been doing

✧

                    Up
      in the sky, bill boards w. rainbow lights
         dominate the city, at least my city

            I compare the fashions,
                                here
                                   &
                                      Margarita/
              I watch my mind, losing
    its precision, Louise just remember, remember your
                           divine
                                intention

NYC 2006

◆

◆

LATIN AMERICA

    The
  GAR ought
 to be ashamed
   O Signora–

No quiero dormir bajo la lluvia
O miss I don't want to sleep in the rain

   Compassion for ALL
              Sentient
                   Beings

       EXCEPT

   O it's beautiful
(la maestra del Tibetano)

❖

      I see the footprints of the dog/then I
            see
                  the
                        dog,

              I wonder

'Will Wittgenstein / solve my problems?' –

SIGNIFICATION & KNOWLEDGE
A Semiotical Analysis of Wittgenstein's work

separates itself fr. stacks of 100's of papers

                &

                f
               a
                l
                 l
                  s

out (of the stack)

             to
               the

                  ground

❖

            Is
             it

    objective or non objective

        WISDOM DISPLAY

                ✧

    I see the foot prints

            I see
              the
               dog/

                ✧

        I hear yr. voice
        00.1.212.222.2016
    Yr. 20,000 miles away but I sit at
            yr. bedside

                &

            commiserate
               w.
                 you

                ✧

A
lady follows me
& says *O I thought*
you were the sister of Che Guevara

You look just like her.
yr.
body
&
everything

No I'm not her/

O I thought you were.

O her name is Helen O she lives in England

Playa Zaragoza,
15.2.06

✧

THE UNKNOWN TOWN

What's between
the lines/ in the window
of
'experience'/ in

'The Mansion of Experience' writes

the
naked
yogin

while
clothed, I, seek to master

the
art
of/
flexibility
&
the
art
of
compassion/

that the window/master
its
own/
light/ frequency
you
take care (taking) images fr. dimensions

(beyond
this
ONE)

&

        sometimes taking
     us for breakfast, the town
                                is
                                          unknown

    where one is *in the presence*
                             of
                               the
                                     mastery

for S & R

❖

❖

CREATURES SAVED

Praying mantis/ stranded at Zaragoza,
crab/ trapped in sand/ big black bug in white cup/
found
in
      forest -

CREATURES KILLED/
An entire family of ants / perhaps HUNDREDS, trapped in
sweater / inadvertently left
      outside
          tent -

Are the Buddhists going to
karma-me-out for this last act/ should I tell
them or just keep quiet, like I've
been about EVERYTHING
these last months

      ✧

I saw
my old friend/ X./ 'does everybody
have to get SENILE' or what ?/ w. EVERYTHING she said I wanted
to disagree but didn't - /I was being 'Buddhist' &/ or Louise polite.

Is this TRAINING for
    a
      poet?

Certainly not

      ✧

It is hard to consider

ENLIGHTENMENT

as a (reasonable) possibility when *sanga itself seems*
so ignorant & cruel / LLL, of course, included
in the mix

✧

Where
has the principle/gone?
Why can't I relate to it, when in one
way or another, I devoted most
of my life
to
it?

✧

✧

ON THE ROAD

which led through the valley,
to the mountain, we two were three, then we
were ONE/ You conducted the
'band'/ as we

escaped generic/ hunger &
discovered a gourmet's delight/ all
our body parts/ transformed/

amid

the

laughter

Pedro Gonzalez
for R & S,

NN

says we were
bodies of light/before/

the food & emotion ruined everything/ I
thought the TANTRIC view was
to enjoy
    the
        'ruin'/

Ati Yogi does not = TANTRA/

Sometimes
I wonder: *what I am doing/
here* / **further** *wld.* BUDDHA

*not be bothered by USA intention to
BOMB THE SHIT out of Iran?/* having
done so already to
    the
        'neighbors'/such

wld. be simply SAMSARA?

that's hard to take/ w. the planet
abt. to auto-destruct

    entirely

◆

The
only happily married
'house holders'/I know

are / GAY. What wld. Buddha say
to that?/ Dalai Lama intervenes in internet
'conversazione' *all relations based on*
affection are valid/ Is ALL this / just THAT ?/ 'samsara' to
Lord Buddha/ if anyone knows, certainly NN does

(but I don't - get it)

In Buddha's time/ there were
ELEMENTS/ rain fell in some kind of
'normal' way/ OK, the Vedas speak about
weather control/ they had missiles which functioned
(probably) a lot better than ours/but
were things really the same/

is samsara = samsara

the only equation?/ I need
to have a dream/ to assure me,

I'm on the
        path
                of
                        light

◇

Sleeping

in green tent/ unexpected night/ all violent/
all strange/ I wake at 4.30/AM trembling/ just then, the
neighbor, passes, also a tent dweller/

the one who has injured my arm weeks before/ (healing session
gone astray/do not trust Russians, like in 2nd grade?

Even MORE terrified/

I get up/ wander off to the guards/ to seek shelter & note:
the STARS/ O infinitely distant & brilliant
stars/ O Earth

YOU ARE REALLY FUCKED UP/

Your inhabitants are so proud
when they have anything (which is nothing)

All you can
think of doing w. yr. man made shit is
KILL & OWN/ (you are so BORING) you

find me outlandish/I find you
                                        boring -

O STARS/ Earth but one
among the many/ we
                  too
                        are
                              aliens/

you are brave to live in a tent at your age

No it is a space ship
&
carries me
to
distant
worlds

✧

✧

        As I wrote, already
                10
                      years
                            ago/

As everyone knows,
**Louise's life is not very economic/ but it cld.
be poetic/ if Love were to**
      penetrate
         her
            solitary
                  condition.

⟡

Reading/
La Vita Nuova/ such
matters are divine reflection/ & can not
be controlled by earthly values, we
can try of course./ but I can't
get back to

((((()))))))))

I think I'm finally writing
'my' book/

A.
said to me, O writing yr. best poems/**I wanted to respond,**
no worst. Leave me alone. **But maybe she**
         was

              e
          f   r
       n   i
     o   n
   c   g
      a
          message

I am treated to an early morning practice
I wish to write to R./ but don't want to aggravate him or
his condition, nevertheless I write this 'ricordo'.

**The black birds
went crazy w. the
raga or jati / DEEPAK/ (just that forbidden one)**

**GGMPNS
SNDPMGRS**

**all gathering, singing, in the Lime Tree/
intoxicated / ecstatic**

THEY WERE 'OUT OF THEIR MINDS'

**I ask myself/ Are these black birds
– in fact – fr. the court of Akbar?**

❖

NOTE: Legend has it that Akbar wished to hear
the forbidden fire raga from his court musician's teacher Haridas.
Haridas didn't want to sing it but finally consented/ then the place burned down, or
almost/ Haridas had trained his daughter to sing the water raga/ so after the fire there
was rain, at least enough to save the musician's (and the king's) life.
There are no further records of the RAGA DEEPAK being
sung at the court of Akbar.

❖

             The
          grey one/ is
      notably absent/ IS the scene
      too 'hysterical' ? / appearing
         (ONLY) /however/

when I return to usual 'morning' practice
         solemn/ Raga TODI/

            S<u>R</u>GMP<u>D</u>NS<u>R</u>
            SN<u>D</u>PM<u>GR</u>S

          As usual listening
    attentively /Grey I have discovered

      is a Mockingbird/ as fascinated
            by Indian Music
                 as
                         I
                            am

                ✧

Feb. 8/

I
am not my
mother to the extent
I am myself – but I am
myself to the extent

I am
my
Mother/
&

still **unable to get
up
to**

TASHIGAR

✧

✧

                    I
                swore the
              white cat slept
    in my tent last night/ green tent/white
              cat/TARA/ a very
                        sensual
                                    'experience'

                        &
              tender/ as well. By
          morning the green tent was
    empty/ but it is a sealed 'affair'/ 'Escape'
          impossible/ for a cat .../ Tell
              me, was this an

        'apparition'/ the famous 'illusion'
            subject of so many texts/
                      but
                still not explaining
              the disappearance of
                      the

                              cat
                      ___

            Believe
                    me
                        Louise

              it is all HOLY, you don't need
                    to look for it/

                      IT IS HERE

                            ✧

        The
body is here & over there
is the music/ or is the music here,
& coalescing, into the music, is my body/ & my body is
the music & my life is the music & the pearl,
the child, all this - the music

at any rate I play it & become it
but not when I am feeling trapped
in someone else's dream & someone else's e-mail
&
someone else's

BEING & many people have felt this & I vowed I wld.
never feel this & I feel it

O what is going
to happen ?

✧

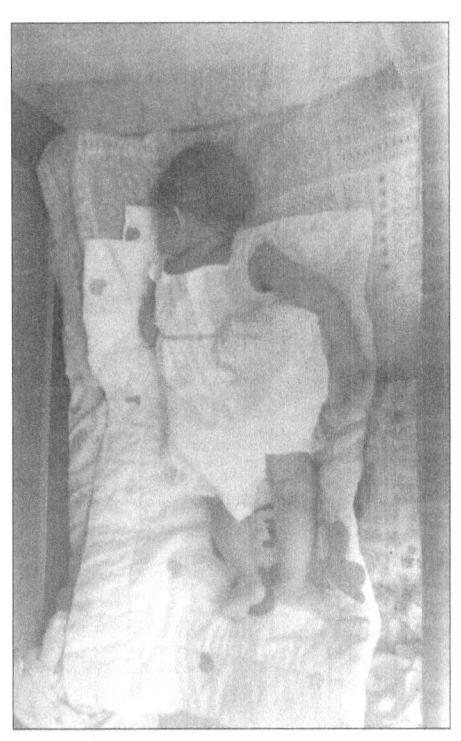

Already

    writing my obituary/strange
abt.
      'impermanence'/ even
              Ira
                &/
                   or

                  La Monte

do not seem to have written theirs *(so far)/*

      ✧

The
obituary changes/
according to mood swings & so forth/

sometimes it's only concerned w. absolute
presence /then it's called 'my'

liberation/

otherwise it is in honor of 'my' great deeds/
which of course obfuscate the terrible ones,

      as
          frequently
                observed/

      ✧

My
obituary
is my poem
Even
as a child/ I found
the death-concept very hard
to swallow/ so I stopped
eating/

now I eat/ but also
write, for instance, my obituary/

still
a
secret
text

✧

✧

              I
        am having
     fun/ being a secret
     heretic/ but it's not
                    just
                       fun/
         I'm
       relieved not to
    be in UGLY *'comedor'* /its pillars
                       w/o
                          a
                             trace

               of
                  Phrygian, Myxolydian

                  or

                       WARMTH

   which every house
              in
                Pedro
                    Gonzalez
     possesses

            (naturally)

              tambien los mas pobres
              (even the most poor)

                    ✧

          Dharma
    can not be force fed

      'I resist & I still resist'
or
   read (about),
              it's
                    in
                        the
                            AIR
    here, absolutely

                ✧

      No body
    ever mentions
the 'rainbow body' of J.C.

          but he
             had
                one

'Non toccarmi' **perce/ niente de toccare**

('Don't touch me' Why not? Nothing to touch.)

          there
           I've
            said
              it

              ✧

         I
    note, the HM
is finally being (properly)

 published exactly 21 years
          after
            1st
                significant

encounter
         w.

           FB / OM TARA TU TARA TURE/

          S
          V
          A
   H
     A
                  ⟡

     Even tho' yr. dead/
   this fruit is still possible
             ⟡
 Judy saw you on the airplane
wing/she was on the way to yr. funeral – You
      said it was very interesting
           to be dead/

       I liked you very
    much (FB) & am glad to
                    have
                      known/

                            you

             ⟡

ALL IN A DAY

3 butterflies/ one yellow & black & useful
for
    avoiding
        H.
(on the path)

A baby lizard who fell fr. a palm tree

(onto me)

&

a chartreuse Praying Mantis,
'on the road'
where
    f
   o
    r
     m
      e
      r
       l
        y

there were Vultures/.

❖

SHINGON

In
the dark pavilion/ I desperately
must speak with the young prince /he waits on the path/
where it is dark,
& no one
will
see/
us

We
speak /the
room is round/ without walls,
without desire/when we separate/
there
is
deep
sadness

he says

*if someone hadn't been waiting
for me we wld. have spoken until dawn*

❖

In
the taxi/
unexpected tears/you travel
to
a
forbidden
city,

a thousand of miles away
I'm
in the front / w. the driver/ playing it

'cool' until I exit/& you leap to the street/ the town celebrating

'The Festival of the Mad'

I'm dressed in white/ it is my festival

&
embrace
me

Soft skin
against my lips, repeated
a thousand years ago, in Japanese temple/ the last farewell.

✧

Sensitive sea/ at dawn

the shore/ deserted/ finally
the vacationing Venezuelans/ have returned
to where they
came
from/

I see a lone pelican/then
large black birds/ in a dense
grey
sky/

when love came, it came

unexpectedly

✧

ALL THAT REMAINS

All that remains of the dark prince
      is
          the
                wrapping – paper:

Ambrofoli GOLDEN MUSS libre de azucar

      &
it's a good thing/

the prince is a 'prick'/ I wisely wrote
in my 12th century Japanese nun's diary/ & last

    night clearly: he's
          a
              'collectioniste'

◆

WHEREAS

Whereas
this morning/ just as I am
playing very nicely to the Lime Trees/

I notice a rather conservative,
certainly elegant little
grey bird, listening

respectfully, obviously a 'connoisseur'

obviously

R.

The 'teachings', the 'Firm' had imperial leanings/ A heretic,
I escape to:
                Palm
                      Tree,
                            at
                                Zaragoza

       ✧

The BEACH is a mess-bottles, wrappings – plastic parts of things/
O this styrofoam/ it's a rock/

       ✧

Water/ Sound/ Silence
SOLITUDE

IT'S A DIVORCE/ whew

       ✧✧✧

       ✧

This morning/ an inventory/ who's over there/

Who's here?

Of course I don't know ALL the people
here, but it seems, over there
        is
            more
              i
               n
                t
                 e
                  r
                   e
                    s
                     t
                      i
                       n
                        g

✧

Playa Zaragoza, Isla. Margarita 2006

" what though my shorts are threadbare
I deserve all your love "

            PW
               after Kakinmoto Hitomaro

✧

THE GAR

Now
I realize
I'm in a Paradise
for POETRY/but what
kind?/ Speaking of hidden readers

& the stacks of chairs are
large looming ghosts/ scaring me
each time/I look up/at them

Meanwhile/
the GUARDS: their rifles
look cinematic enough but even if
I placate them w. Coca Cola/ will they
SPARE me? / *Policia* wander thru Dharma Pure Land/

either they're lost
or
we
are,

PW
still cheering me/ tho

(only apparently)
dead

❖

Poor/MASTER, w. all these
strange troubled

disciples/ I'm glad
not to be one of them
(almost) or not for long/ GET
                OUT
                  OF
                    MY
                      WAY

I have things to do & will meet you /later

The WORLD is a big place & I have appointments/
especially w. my music teacher, *so there*

❖

❖

Today
I sang Father Death Blues
to the galloping waves/

then faithful R. cheers me w.
                               a

                                    poem –

Across even small distances such
acts have strong power/ elated

white cat & I enjoy
the sounds of

       f
     a
    l
     l
      i
       n

          g

        rain

✧

                    Everyone
            or almost everyone/ certainly
         poets/ need a muse/ *tertons* need them
          too & often, in failure to find them,
                do not produce their /
                       ter/ &
                              so
                                 w.
                                    poets

                whereas I have not had
              what I planned/ certainly as
            a child, at least certain figures at certain
         intervals do lend to me their inspiration, via such
                refined imagining, if not
                              (entirely)
                                    their
                                          ear

                    &

              hats off to Leonardo/
           for inventing, among so many other
               things/ less important perhaps,

                    the bicycle/ I think
                    sailing down the road

                       this evening's

                             old
                              moon

                                    full

                              ❖

My mother lies
in her card board
box coffin/ surrounded
by flowers/ I chose
especially,

her dress is NOT one,
of course NOT, she (or I) might
have
chosen,

A

thousand strange remarks,
& harsh statements, a
beating or 2 or 10
or 20/
ALL
BURN
w.
her/

✧

Only feelings
reserved /in my bones
do not go up in flames, are
not buried/ in a cemetery
in
Brooklyn

No I feed them
they grow – entire

gardens have been constructed/

      even forests in which shyly
       but in deep resonance,
            we
                  meet/
                        again,

      w. no speech, not
     even bodies, deformed &
       by whose hand,
       to complicate
                the

              AROMA

          ✧

            &

      the music/
   connoisseurs & artists,
    players, all upon
            this
                tuneful
                    planet,

  whirling about/

dancing, it's fabulous the FAITH I've
       conjured up/
           this

                 morning

        ✧

GOING AROUND THE WORLD

*It's
a once in a
lifetime experience* **explains a rather large/
but charming lady – on her beach chair-**

*at least for me, some
people have done it 5 or 6 x
already*

**& I retreat to ARSH 10247 to read
Hakim Bey & the old abbot**

**still with us/
w.
me**

'GONE GONE into the cool O MAMA'

✧

✧

Tripping
on the way to the
lady's house/ on my paralyzed left
arm/ chiropractory gone, wrong/ very wrong/

moaning I arrive to be (unexpectedly) 'soothed'
by Sai Baba's *vibhuti*/ I promise him to
desist fr. my dope & continue
on my way

Not that I have PARTICULAR faith, in the
saint, especially in his NEW
        AGE
          form

yet he appears/ &
on several occasions, at least
has set the
    situation/
      straight.

Can I ask for more?

❖

dope: in this case, pain killing injection, administered,
at the hospital in Juan el Griego - at my request

LA M & M

      Butterflies
  keep dropping on my

SARANGI, while bombs

    keep falling on
             people's
                    heads

Dear Teachers –

    Can
      you

        explain

          this
          to
            me?

✧

BRASS BAND/
for

La Virgine del Vale/ Charito,
fr. the playa,
　　　　　is

transformed: a BHAKTI

in ecstasy, she leads
　　　　the
　　　　　　procession

which I 'accidentally'
　　(&
　　　not
　　　　really)

encounter, on my
　　　　way

　　　　　　home

❖

GUARDANA DEL DIBUJO

ZARAGOZA SUN

on Xmas day – the *playa's*
like an incredible café
in
Amsterdam

lots of people
&
NO
    paranoia

Except perhaps
for students of NN
         who
           stay
             away

fr. the 'locals'.

You see people, of all kinds here, the woman in
white w. her great granddaughter, fr. LA.
& so many others

✧

        She's
     sincere &
harmless/ scraps of last
night's poetry/ floating in the
grass/ 'it's mine' she says / reaching down–

unmistakable / her black scrawl on white
               paper, wet
                            w.
                                      morning dew/

      why, it's a poem for R.

                 ✧

But
      is it mine or anyone's?/

At the back of the Restaurant,
noisy party, in front, sudden
      inspiration ——

                 ✧

      Who
    says 'Sex'
  is only for the young/
this time Guru's got it wrong –

party over & I'm soon to go / back
                                up
                             to
                                  windy
                                        mt.

dangerous & THE ROADS/are

       falling a
               p
                 a
                   r
                     t

WHO's TO SAY – *it's mine*

       ✧

Good Acts in Pedro Gonzalez/

Will a bicycle make her happy — will the towers
rise again/ will J.
                a

                          p

                        p

              e

                a

                        r
                              miraculously

Do you really expect me to answer these questions???

HOW ARE YOU?

I'm going to CUBA
without passing go -

Mind relaxing/ but is it?
by listening? by paying attention to the
details?/ A local lady makes a Ganesh out
of shells/ tho her roof
         is
           falling
                  down

'O that stuffs fr. China'

The DREAM of China

No hope for Louise
but really, no/
        fear
            either.

Playa Zaragoza 3 l.1.2006

✧

✧

                It's
                 a
            relief to hear
           the concert of RN &
          to find myself worrying abt.
         where I'm going to sleep tonite
            & not whether or not
                 you
                   will
                      live/

                     I'll never forgive you if you don't
Amsterdam 1991

                         ✧

                    You
              died/ I sucked
         in the prana of the UNIVERSE/
    It wasn't easy/ I traveled great distances/ often mapless,

                         At
             last/ I found you/ you lived
    in the sonority of the notes that pursued me/ yr. pulse
                         in
                            timeless
                                   time/
                                       the
                                          '*tal*'

                         ✧

                 I found no difference
                    between you &
                        the
                            SOUND/

                         ✧

       Maybe I'm crazy/
 now, or just more disciplined/

 but the music rose to a new
       level & it wasn't

            by
                 chance

               ✧

           Not
       that I invited
    you/ yet you appeared/
       VOICE / beyond
         fork/ front
           Wingèd

               ✧

           These
           people
        have nothing
                 in
                     common /

 just teachings abt. visions
                     &
                         rainbows.

El Munequito Pampator 4.06.06

               ✧

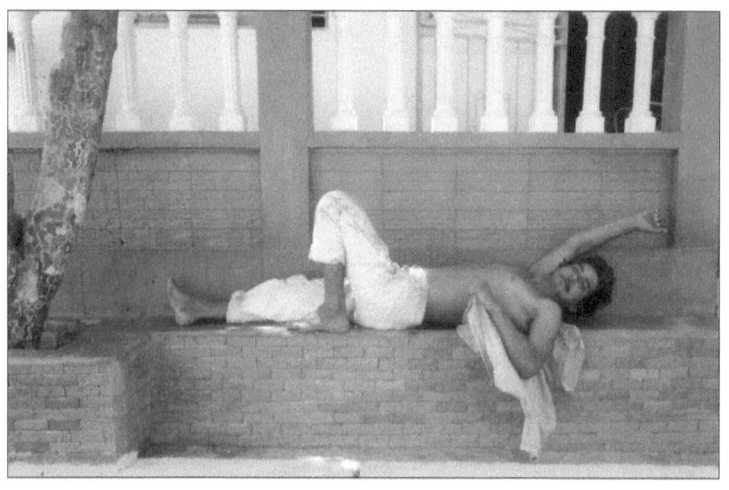

                              A

                  certain obsession w.
                  Bellini / & the young men
                                          of

                                                  Memling/

                  Painterly occupations/ the male
                      homosexual/ object of/
                                          Romantic/
                                                  Muse /

    not

                  in Bellini of course, he liked/ not

                      the boys of the tavern

                                      but

                                              Madonnas

                                  ✧

MESSAGE TO ADOLESCENT POETS by SAINT POL –ROUX

Magnificent pilgrim in memory's palms
Pelerin magnifique en palmes de memoire

O your nude feet on the blasphemy of the bargemen,
(O tes pieeds nus sur le blaspheme des rouliers

Ignore the spit spattered in the book of spells
Neglige les crachats epars dan le grimoir

Injustice of the toads that for you are shoes
Injuste des crapauds qui te sont des souliers.

Unwrapping your rosy clock of existence,
Enlincelant ta rose horloge d'existence

Evoke your phantom at the table of the mad
Evoque ton fantome a la table des fols

And divide his eagle on wings of distance
Et partage son aigle aux ailes de distance

In order to tame the sun flower's faith
Afin d'apprivoiser la foi des tournesois.

From there, mercy in the good pleats of the cottage
De la, misericorde aux bons plis de chaumiere

With a rose – trellis forehead and hollyhock mouth,
Avec un front de treille et la bouche tremeire,

Adopts the old wolves who bleat through the fields.
Adopte les vieux loups qui belent par les champs

And regenerates their pupil in pain,
Et regenere leur prunelle douloureuse

To the diamond that laughs in the nugget of time
Au diamant qui rit dans la houille des temps

Like the flowering agate of a she-cat in love.
Comme l'agate en fleur d'une chatte amoureuse.

❖

Translation: Daniel Abdal Hayy Moore & LLL (via e-mail)
Isla Margarita, 2005

Isla M

I
got some
extra $$$ & bought a few
Madonnas fr. a poor local girl who
likes
NN

◆

One
fell out of my purse
& broke her head. Next I lost my shawl.
No permanence here

◆

Is the yellow butter-

fly

J.

maybe

◆

Death

is conventional,
everyone dies

mother
      father
            f
         l

          o
            w

              e

                r

&

fish

except some beings like Changchub Dorje

Philip Whalen
has to die,
     too

I wish he didn't & cld. put on his

eye glasses

✧

I just have to become the most powerful possible version of myself

                 it is bound to
                             happen
   As
    I write I feel my heart
                         grow

                         l

                           i

                         g
                      h

                      t

                           e

                         r

          I find Esther
          kind Queen

     I find myself in the flowers

I'm all covered up/ Namkhai Norbu, if you can't
          MAKE ME BLOOM

          No one can

✧

End Poems

...I hesitated to admit them but they didn't want to be disregarded
so I included them for the discerning reader whom they may have wanted to contact despite my judgement.

❖

Strange how the poems disappear/ finally I write something -
- enthusiastically & it disappears/ I guess I shld. go
to the GAR...so many people here tonight

Wrote to R, finally, honestly-
nature of mind, nature of luminosity, how near, how far?

Where is the poem?

I just
wrote abt. this & so many subjects/
crazy computer self-erases,

Nature of mind/of
luminosity, if you're always
present, why must I cultivate you or
search for you? If you are the 10th state

Why can't I relax?

If I see the dancers in the
Shingon temple, what's the problem?

Great luminous
mind stream

Anthurium, Heliconia &
Passion Flowers, at Esther's
before New Year

2006

Bananas, Pomengranates/

I,

go swimming
the long distance. way out, to sea
far
out

to see a crab, a school of
fish
literally,

NY City Ramblers/ what's
all this stuff in my mind/sold 12 books,

Bananas, Pomengranates, Papayas

antiques of all sorts/
stars even

I'm
looking better/ my mosquito attackers
have subsided, time to go back to retirement home, the GAR,
seat of liberation/

Master's Mind

✧

I go to the empty palace/ my harp has reached the
Royaume des Oiseaux

◇

I approach the circular hall,
A sheet of paper lies in the grass soaked in the fluids
of the night. I recognize the script as my own & find a poem
I have hastily written the night before

"...Thought I had
lost you/ not a ROMANTIC/ but a
life line/ The King's scribe, the Queen's messenger,
her lover the most radiant
in le corps that guards
the
treasury,

I, a stranger, found
fellowship at festivities
in secret honor of the ancestors, in secret honor
of the
Master's
Word.

In secret I strung
a string of pearls in your honor/

◇

In secret I sent prayers
to protect your portion of the Domain,
In secret I sang
                    for
                         yr.

                                  respite"

◇

Other
verses appeared in my mind/the
King's initiation/demanding less/than a moment
in the mirror
of
reflection/

Hardly had I looked into the mirror, when your shadow appeared/
in the dream

sequence, my friend, lay in state,
&
you
comforted
me

✧

✧

Playa Zaragoza
All 'those ancient Chinamen'

My father/
in my dream/
shows me his NEW horoscope/ A map
to
locate
him/

❖

I wonder if
HM

saved my life/ I dream
of a large painting last night
which seems to be his/ would be his,
but isn't - I feel the time
of finishing this work
is
at
hand/

Valery: You do not finish a translation. You abandon it

❖

Pedro Gonzalez 2005

nb. Henri Michaux. See www.milkmag.org for translation LLL

I still think X. was ideal for
J's departure/ he was going to die anyway, that
was clear - **at least he died, well protected, in his world view**
until he hit the bardo of course but also, as a musician,
he got to make a kind of step,

I

hope

he is *Safe in Heaven Dead* (re: Kerouac)

❖

Last night I dream of his mother / We're in the dimension
of the Power Puff Girls/ there's a confrontation
&
suddenly
I'm flying through the sky -
she can also fly
but
I am faster
& escape her

❖

I see that same gray bird/
he waits on the path/
when I practice
music/

I
hear
the
myriad

song

❖

LA M & M

Butterflies
keep dropping on my

SARANGI while bombs

keep falling on
people's
heads. Dear
Teachers
    can
        you

    explain this
            to
                me?

✧
As
I contemplate
the richness of yr. love
all the while wondering why
the tortoises in my bathtub still have
not taught me

the perfect allegories
of Dream
    &
        Intonation

✧

                    While
                we await the
            metaphoric collapse/
            of the vast metropolis
             in which our highest
                 aspirations
                        were assembled / an entire
            species facing extinction
                as we sing
                        of
                            the

MIRACULOUS

            Here, in the Vestige of
                Prayer & Incantation
                    still,
                        gathered,
                                the
                                    flock,
                the wild birds, the
                            ancients
                                    understood

                as the butteflies
                as the bombs

                                f
                                e
                                l
                                l

Bagnore 2005

⋄

                    In
              frail morning,
          the simplistic/window,

     the experience of Sensation, sen-
       sational NEWS, the Americans
            want the oil of Irak.
             Saudi Arabian oil
                    Is

                        not

                            enough
                                for
                                    us

     We want oil. We are all Americans.

                    Only
               the Parakeet,
             seen in the park,
              dares to leave
                        its
                            cage

            I am a light in the darkness

                            ✧

Pedro Gonzalez 2004

The
house
finally falls

in
Pedro
Gonzalez,

& no one 'minds' in fact, there's
a
party, of sorts

❖

Behind the façade, twisted weeds/ trees & flowers

❖

The hairdresser, a cross dresser, of course
& friends have set up a table
&
sip tea
with great elegance

in

front

of

the

'ruin'

❖

In a thousand years
it will all be dust, in ruins or buried like
the Tun Huang Caves, but

now everyone's
concerned
(abt. the Gar)

◆

All this building up & decaying...

◆

I'm gonna
circle the stupa

(but
    which
        way?

                Louise

which

way?)

◆

Passion Flowers

among the weeds – on
the way to
the

kitchen
at
Tashigar Norte

✧

Pain & indecision/

leaving
retreat/

Mosquito sanga
surrounds me/ beneath

Coconut trees
at
Zaragoza.

Pedro Gonzalez 2004

✧

Earthquakes, that are not

earthquakes,

Disease, famine & plague
which are not

these/

these/times, the end
of the kalpa, the end of the calendar,
the end

of/

dream

❖

The Terton & The Ter

The Tibetan alphabet offers unique opportunities to unique beings who are called, in the tradition - Tertons. Said to be among the 25 close disciples of the great master Guru Padmasambhava (8th century AD), with whom these teachings are said to have originated, the tertons, upon perception of certain mystic letters & signs, in dream, in space or in other dimensions, are recipients of entire texts - stored within these letters (or signs) intact. Rediscovered, they are transcribed to benefit sentient beings in general & in particular to benefit those in the direct company of the terton master.

The reception of such text requires, for both terton & terton*ma* (i.e. both male & female of the genre) an appropriate consort. The bliss that is generated through the union of these two develops & sustains the clarity with which the text is evoked, invoked & ultimately transcribed. Written in poetic scripture these 'sadhanas' lead to the liberation of those who have the capacity & conditions to follow them.

In the Western canon, although such lineages (of rediscovered text) are lost, the intrinsic divinity of love & its evocative power have clearly manifested. In the 12th century, Dante Alighieri summons his muse. AMORE will instruct & then release the poet's passion & his bliss. In *Il Dolce Stil Novo* - the adoration of the beloved is transported fr. 'religious' confine to a courtly or even purely personal domain. Love as divine apprehension is a sustained theme in the poetic canons & hermeticism (*The poem does not lie to us. We lie under its law* [*]) of the West & is maintained in the 21st century, despite the revolution in form in modern & post-modern genre.

The Book L written while poet LLL camps out, hangs around near & participates in the '*mandala*' of the 21st century Terton Choegyal Namkhai Norbu can be seen as a juxtaposition of these 2 traditions & their potential - for greater detail, please consult the poet's essay online at www.bigbridge.org THE YELLOW SCROLL

The poems in The Book L. were written, for the most part in 2006, on Isla Margarita, located, in the Caribbean, just east of Caracas. Revolutionary zeal, utopian mysticism & tradition, both Spanish-Catholic & Buddhist, characterize the ambient & aspiration of LLL who attempts to resuscitate the only yoga she recognizes as 'untaught' - the old one, of poesie.

> *'if I don't write poetry, what do I do?'*
> NN

LLL NYC 2008

* *John Wieners*
A Poem for Vipers

GLOSSARY

1. **BHAKTI** (skt) fr. the root *bhaj*, to share – the love of god - *bhakta*, one who has such feelings. Bhakti yoga is the yoga that liberates through love. Existing in all traditions, Chaitanya was a great Indian exponent, St. John of the Cross & St. Christina The Astonishing in the Christian tradition.

2. **CHANGCHUB DORJE:** (1826-1961/1978) The master of Namkhai Norbu Rinpoche, he established 'The Community of Liberation' in East Tibet & acting as a 'barefoot doctor' was not perceived as a spiritual master by the Chinese who would have eliminated him if he were so perceived. A disciple of Nyala Pema Dundu & Adzom Drukpa he is the root Guru of Namkhai Norbu Rimpoche who met him, at the age of 17, one year after a clear dream of him. A non-literate, Changchub Dorje dictated extensive medical texts to NN who was his assistant at the time, including a cure for AIDS, a disease he said (in the 1950's) which wld. manifest in the future. The death of the master has not really been determined. Namkai Norbu wrote that *for me, my master never died*. It is reported that the manifestation of his 'rainbow body' was interrupted.

3. **CHE GUEVARA**: (1928-1967) Argentinean doctor, traveler, orator & diarist, Che was a political theorist (see his seminal *Guerilla Warfare*) & fighter (later commandante) in Fidel Castro's July 26th Revolutionary army. He held various positions in the new government (Minister of Industry & President of the National Bank) until 1965 when, as a clandestine & revolutionary, he left first for Congo & then Bolivia. Che Guevera was captured & executed, with the assistance of the CIA, under the orders of Bolivian President Rene Barrento. *'The new man will be driven by moral rather than material incentives.'* His iconic image is prominently displayed in Margarita Island (& everywhere else) on walls, doors, windows, buses, towels & hats.

4. **FATHER DEATH BLUES** – Allen Ginsberg's (1928-1997) great hymn to his father - written in an airplane, flying to his funeral *'genius death your work is done, lover death, your body's gone, father death I'm coming home'*.

5. **FB:** Franco Beltrametti (1938-1995) Swiss poet & artist who lived a hermetic life in Riva San Vitale, SV. A master of 'poesia viseva' (visual poetics), he collaborated w. many poets: Tom Rayworth, Dario Villa Adriano Spatola & Giulia Nicolai (Tam-Tam & edizions Geiger), James Koller (Coyote Press), Annabel Levitt (Vehicle editions) musicians: Steve Lacy, Joelle Leandre, Demetrius Stratos, & artists: Giovanni Augstino, PAM & Brion Gysin. He was the author & maker of numerous books – in Italian & English. Fondazione Franco Beltrametti welcomes poets to his extensive library, housed in the courtyard where FB lived & worked the last decades of his life. (*qui ha fatto centro della sua maginalita* G. Pozzi.)

6. **GANESH**: The son of the divine pair Shiva & Parvati, Ganesh has a human form & an elephant's head. As patron of Letters, he dictates the Indian Epics (*Mahabharata & Ramayana*) to Vlamiki, their scribe. He who removes obstacles, assures beginnings & purifies all tasks, Ganesh is worshipped by Hindus, Jains & Buddhists alike. A self-originated Ganesh recently reported (by the NY Post) in Brooklyn, NY – in the form of a plant protruding fr. a fence, cured of all ills those who perceived it.

7. **GAR**: (tib.) A meeting place (for practitioners), (skt.) *ghar* = home. Namkhai Norbu organized several for the benefit of his ('homeless') students. No one lives at the gars permanently but students gather there for retreats & practice. Tashigar, No. on Margarita Island, VE (*What are the conditions for disseminating the Longsal on Margarita Island? 'Totally perfect'* replies the Queen of the Dakinis) & Merigar, in C. Italy, regarded at its inception as 'an ornament of the teaching' are two of them.

8. **GIOVANNI BELLINI**: (1430-1518) Venetian painter, teacher of Giorgone & Tiziano, brother in law of Andrea Mantegna, his Madonnas are masterworks of the high Renaissance. HANS MEMLING (1430-1494) was born in the Netherlands, he lived & painted in Bruges, Belgium. The last major artist of the high Renaissance in the Low Lands, he is considered to be the successor of Van Eyck (see Het Lam Gods http://www.katapi.org.uk/Art/AdorationLamb.html) & Roger v. der Weyen.

9. **HAKIM BEY**: aka Peter Lamborn Wilson (1945 -) Scholar of esoteric Islam, political philosopher & historian, translator & poet, PLW developed theories of onto-logical anarchism in books which are classics for the counter culture of the 20th & 21st. century. See *TAZ, Temporary Autonomous Zone, Shower of Stars, Pirate Utopias, Green Hermeticism, Avant Gardening, The Sacred Drift* & most recently the poetry books *Queer Rain, Atlantis & Black Fez Manifesto &t.*

10. **HM**: Henri Michaux (1898-1984) Born in Brussels, Michaux lived & worked, for the greater part of his life, in Paris. Poet, painter & sage, a modest interpretor of oriental culture, he is widely regarded as a master of 20th century European writing. for LLL's transl. fr. the French - see Toward Totality Shivastan Press 2006 & online: http://www.longhousepoetry.com/landeslevi.html & www.milkmag.com, no. 4.

11. **LA M & M:** La Monte Young (1935 -) & Marian Zazeela (1940 -) **D**isciples of Pandit Pran Nath, La Monte & Marian direct the Kirana School of Music. La Monte Young, recognized (along w. colleague Terry Riley & Italian composer, Giancinto Scelsi) for monumental contribution to the Western understanding of Just Intonation, sustained intervals & the drone, is also revered as the grandfather of ambient rock. Marian Zazeela, the beautiful muse of Jack Smith (Flaming Creatures)is a calligrapher, light artist & creator of the installations in which the

compositions of La Monte Young are performed (see The Well Tuned Piano, DVD & The Dream House, 275 Church St., NYC).

12. **LA VITA NUOVA**: (It.) Dante Aligieri's 12th century masterpiece on the nature of poetics & love. The poetry *A ciascun'alma presa, e gentil core, nel cui cospetto ven lo dir presente, in ciò che mi rescrivan suo parventesalute in lor segnor, cioè Amore* in this classic treatise is dictated by Amore who manifests fr. the divine realm on behalf of the poet, henceforth his intermediary. According to Il Dolce Stil Novo, the beloved introduces the divine understanding & the capacity to exalt this understanding in the iconic poem or song. The poem, in the tradition, is a conduit to & from the divine word although not its exact reflection.

13. **LEONARDO DA VINCI:** (1452-1519) Philosopher, painter, inventor, mathematician, musician. & vegetarian. Illegitimate son of Piero da Vinci & servant girl Catherine, Leonardo is rumored to have died in the arms of King Francois I. Inventor of the bicycle, the helicopter & numerous other devices, some say he was a time traveler, predicting, in his extensive journals, the collapse of civilization due to man's insensitivity & cruelty to his natural habitat.

14. **LUDWIG WITTGENSTEIN:** (1889-1951) Austrian Philosopher, who w. his Tractatus-Logico-Phiosophicus revolutionized 20th century logistic thinking. A professor, a schoolteacher, an architect, a writer, a patron to poets, a hermit, his philosophic analysis is unsurpassed & its influence, with the passage of time, undiminished. The youngest of 4 sons, he is the only one to have lived into adulthood. Seeking an ultimate logic, he arrived at a theory similar to the Buddhist one of emptiness despite his intention. *"There is a very practical aspect to your attitude in general."* Cage: *"Right I think that the determinist position is very much related to a lot of occidental thinking, which moves toward a goal, which is non-existent; one goes toward a centre, toward an idea. In the Zen point of view, every sound is at the centre so you have a multiplicity of centers. That's all Zen is, there's nothing peculiar about it." "Yeah I know you're very influenced by oriental philosophy, but I've also heard you mention your interest in Wittgenstein, for instance how do you stand in general to occidental philosophy?" "Well I like Wittgenstein mainly because of the language, which I think is very beautiful. And his strong relation to Buddhism, which isn't expressed in those words. One can become empty and I think that a lot of Wittgenstein for instance, moves in that direction."* Fr. an interview w. John Cage.

15. **NAMKHAI NORBU RINPOCHE**: (1938 -) ATI Yoga Master, also a terton, capable of receiving & transmitting entire teachings received through self-manifesting letters & signs. At first criticized for his teachings of Dzog-Chen or Ati Yoga (see above) in the West, he is now recognized as an outstanding Dzog Chen Master. Author of numerous texts on this ancient tradition, he is revered by his 20th century students as a Nirmanakaya form of the Buddha. *'a light in the time of darkness'* - is an epithet for himself he found in a rediscovered text*(see p.86)*.

16. **OM TARA TU TARA TURE SVAHA**.(skt.) The mantra (the subtle or *sthula* form in Sanskrit epistemology) of the goddess TARA. In her white form, Goddess of compassion, in her green form, Goddess of enlightened activity, Tara is considered to have 21 iconic forms, each one of which represents a different aspect of her capacity.

She is the female form of the Avolekiteshvara, the Buddha of Compassion & emerged fr. one of his tears (see p. 44).

17. **PHRYGIAN & MIXOLODIAN:** (grk.) Pythagorean modes, established by Greek mathematician & philosopher Pythagoras (6 BC), w. the same notation as Indian ragas, Bhairavi & Kamaj. Some of the modes, i.e. Dorian & Ionian, in this system were also the names of Ancient Greek architectural columns.

18. **PW:** Philip Whalen (1923-2002) Poet, Zen master, connoisseur of food & verse, Philip Whalen figures prominently in the work of Gary Snyder & Jack Kerouac (*The Dharma Bums*) & was a reader at the seminal reading '6 Poets at Gallery 6', North Beach, San Francisco,1956. *The best music I make myself. Quite seriously the best is my own, heard in dream.*

19. **RAGA:** (skt). rage or passion. A system of musical exposition whose basis is 5, 6 or 7 ascending & descending 'swaras' or notes. Subdivided into microtones of which there are 22 in the natural scale (& up to 84 in more esoteric instruction) all aspects of raga relate to specific elements, planets & humors, to the time of day, the season & to the ancient theory of aesthetics RASA. The *raga* classification is relatively new, codified, in our times by Vishnu Narayan Bhatkandhe *(Hindustani Sangeet Paddhati)* whereas the *jatis* date fr. the medieval era. Todi, **s r flat g flat m raised, p d flat n s** is a solemn morning raga fr. the former system whereas Deepak, the fire raga, is from the later. **Sa re ga ma pa dha ni sa** (s r g m p d s) are the names of the notes, each is related to an animal cry, as well as to the above characteristics. Sangeet or music was capable of liberating both player & listener *'uniting player & public in a single moment of consciousness'* (see RASA by Rene Daumal, transl. LLL, Shivastan Press 2003).

20 **RAINBOW BODY**: (tib. *ja lus*) – Indicating total liberation fr.the mortal situation, he or she who attains the rainbow body has dissolved his or her elements into their natural bliss & clarity, leaving no sign (or body) at death. There are some examples in our modern times & many in antiquity (see Mira Bai, *Sweet On My Lips*. Cool Grove. Pr. 2009) fr. diverse traditions.

21. **SAI BABA OF SHIRDI**: (ca.1835-1918) Appearing in Shirdi, in the 19th century, this saint integrated Muslim & Hindu worlds & taught a single truth to both communities. Revered, by some, as an incarnation of Kabir, the medieval poet-saint, who, to avoid conflicts between his Muslim & Hindu constituents, turned at his death, into flowers. Sai Babas of Shirdi, in an ordinary seated position, is iconographically present throughout India. Sai Baba of Hyderabad, (1929 -) his supposed reincarnation, is famous for *vibhuti* or self-originating red ash & other objects manifested for the benefit of his disciples. Both are considered *siddhas* or fully realized by those who are devoted to them.

22. **SAINT POL-ROUX**: (1869-1941) A symbolist poet (& writer, principally of

opera), he frequented the salon of S. Marllame & was patronized by Sarah Bernhardt for whom he wrote *la Dame a la Faux*. With the proceeds of his libretto *To Louise*, he moved to Provence. His seaside villa, a center for literary activity was vandalized in 1940 and shortly thereafter burned to the ground. St. Pol-Roux died of cardiomyopathy, a broken heart. His works were posthumously published by his daughter, Divine. In his *Vague de Reves* 'Wave of Dreams' Louis Aragon describes the mania for dreaming that spread over Paris in the late 19th century: Saint Pol-Roux before going to bed in the early hour of the morning put up a notice on his door *'poet at work'*. Walter Benjamin, Archive.

23. **SAMSARA**: (skt) the world as it is perceived through the dualistic perception of our ignorance. **NIRVANA**: (skt) the world in its revealed aspect, without subject or object or judgment to distract from the natural state of contemplation. Both samsara & nirvana are understood to be 'ornaments' of enlightened mind.

24. **SARANGI**: (skt.) sa-100, rang-color. Instrument of 100 colors, the sarangi is a bowed harp whose predecessors are found in both Afghanistan (Sarinda) & Sri Lanka (Ravenatha). Originally a liturgical instrument, keeping both rhythm (*tal*) & melody (*swar*), the instrument was associated in So. India w. the temples & later, in No. India, during the British rule, w. the brothels. In the 20th century principally through the extraordinarily gifted Bundu Khansahib (see www.sarangi.info/sarangi), it became a concert instrument. Bundu Khan was often found playing for flowers instead of, as scheduled, in concert halls. Pandit Ram Narayan (RN) is a contemporary master.

25. **SHINGON**: (chin.) A Tantric school of Japanese Buddhism, Shingon was introduced in the Heian period (794-1185) by the Monk Kukai who studied tantric practice (804-806) in China. The central deity is Buddha Vairocana, the white A is a symbol of & vehicle to the 'state' (of illumination) & all prayers, as in the Tibetan tantric schools, are in Sanskrit. The lineage of instruction is Indian in origin as are the deities depicted in the iconography.

26. **TANTRA**:(skt.) continuity, tantric adj. In India, the body of knowledge heretic to the Brahmanic texts & requiring a Guru for application & practice. In Tibet, the body of knowledge contained in & transmitted through the elements directly & NOT through the oral teachings of Sakyamuni Buddha. Tantric practice, in both regions, relies on mudra & mantra whereas Ati Yoga is the direct, mind-to-mind path whose support is the natural presence or state of the practitioner.

27. **TERTON**:(tib). or tertonma, feminine. In the Tibetan Buddhist tradition, all tertons (& tertonmas) are associated w. the great master Guru Padmasambhava, who introduced Buddhism to Tibet and with whom these texts or 'ters' are said to have originated. The tertons rediscover 'terma' (or 'texts' or 'teachings') in their mind streams, but also, in rocks, trees & the empty sky. The TER are stored in individual letters, when 'deciphered' entire texts are revealed & then recorded by he or she who receives them.

The terma, which was taught on Margarita island, is called *The Innermost Essence of the Dakinis of the Luminous Clarity of the Universe*.

28. **UNUSUAL EARTHQUAKES**: A reference to the earthquake recorded beneath Manhattan Island shortly after 9.11 & considered by some to have been a 'bomb' beneath the city. Nicolas Tesla, in 1912, induced. fr. his home on 46 E. Houston, the first simulated event of this sort, his experiments were unfortunately appropriated by the US military-see http://www.fromthewilderness.com/free/pandora/haarp.html. Unusual Famines: Those produced by deliberate mismanagement of food & money, resulting in sustained deprivation for the impoverished & great profit for the instigators of such deliberation.

29. **VIRGEN DEL VALLE**: (Sp) The Virgin of the Valley unites the Catholic Madonna (introduced by the conquering Spanish in the 1600s) & the native or tribal goddess La Vagina Dentata, a ferocious form of the female deity, The Virgin (see. p. 7) is dressed in white & depicted without child. She wears a crown whose shape, according to Namkhai Norbu Rinpoche is that of a half vajra. She is patron saint & protector of Isla Margaritsa - *dile a la Virgen del Valle que yo en su manto me escudo*.

Louise Landes Levi – poet & translator, musician & traveler. Born on Manhattan Island, she now lives in Bagnore, GR. Italy & on an island to the East of Caracas, Isla Margarita. (*see* 'My Journals' *The Book L* homepage. www.coolgrove.com)

Recent publications:
Banana Baby - w. facing Italian translations by A. Tuoni Super Nova 2006
Toward Totality (Henri Michaux) transl. LLL fold-out I & II Longhouse 2005 & Shivastan 2006
Don't Fuck w. the Airlines Il Bagatto 2005
Avenue A & Ninth Street Shivastan 2003
Ma'Kar A Kar/MA Il Begatto 2002
Chorma - w. facing Italian translation by S. Rigori Porto dei Santi 2000
Forthcoming: Crazy Louise or La Conversazione Sacra (Il Begatto), Ma'Kar A Kar'MA, (Univ. of Rhode Island, Fine Arts Books) & The Deep Diamond, a broadside, Shivastan 2009

Online works:
On the Islands w. Norbu Rinpoche 2005 www.unlikelystories.org
HO (Parto Venerdi) 2004 www.bigbridge.org
Banana Baby 2003 www.poeticinhalation.com, ed. Andrew Lundwall
Chorma 2000 www.portodeisanti.org
The Highway Queen 1994 www.genabrink.com - originally a map, il Bagatto w. Post-Buddhist-Punk, Vienna. ed. S. Peddi (refer www.bigbridge.org/contributors for access)
Celestial Graffiti www.poetz.com an anthology ed. Ira Cohen
& selected poetry at www.unlikelystories.org, www.otoliths.blog.com, www.luxlotus.com, www. deepcleveland.com, www.jackmagazine.com et.al.

A founding member of Daniel Moor's Floating Lotus Magic Opera Company - instrumental recordings: **Kinnari, Padma & Kyerang,** Music for Meditation & Spoken Art Recordings: **Kunst is die Liefde in Elke Daad** w. Simon Vinkenoog & **Oasis**, w. J. Bishop O'Brien.

Since 1992 director of Il Bagatto Books, printing occasional chapbooks, broadsides & postcards. Please contact the author for any publications or recordings that are as difficult to find as she is: levitate108@hotmail.com. For more complete bibliography & biographical details, please see www.coolgrove.com/book & http://www.bigbridge.org/issue 10/bios.htm

Cool Grove Press has published **Guru Punk** (1999) & **Sweet On My Lips The Love Poems of Mira Bai** 1997 & 2003.

For the author's THANGKAS & TANKS, please see
Book L. homepage. www.coolgrove.com

ACKNOWLEDGMENTS

One morning, in Tashigar, on Margarita island, I gave some thought to the word, *elohim*. I tried to visualize the word. It means, in Hebrew - 'god' or 'grace'. That same morning, when a sudden downpour interrupted my walk, I took refuge beneath the veranda of a house in the village, the poor village, just opposite the Gar. A very beautiful man, I noticed at once that he looked exactly like the young Jack Kerouac, handed me a book. 'Read this' he said which was odd, because most of the people living opposite the gar are non-literate - it is only w. the Chavez innovations that the villagers can go to school. He handed me his bible. Kerouac, as an older man, I remember, was a religious Catholic. To my astonishment I can read the Spanish text & I, of course, open the book, to a page w. the word *elohim* gracefully written out - in Hebrew - amidst the narrative.

One's friends, those who are manifest & those who are hidden support the grace waves of all works. I wld. like to thank Lee Ann Brown & Sylvie Degliez, Bob Arnold & Jonathan Penton for useful suggestion, Michael Rothenberg & Cralan Kelder for editorial perspicuity, Ira Cohen for reminding me that I can not write prose (which is an indirect appreciation of my poetry, seldom offered & never by myself to myself). I also thank DS who suffered my presence in his already too small room, 1 hr. fr. Manhattan, Jesus, who protected me fr. the managers of the PMU café on Avenue A & all the unnamed ones, as important as those named.

To the *sangha*, my apologies if I have gone too far. Remember, all this represents my mind stream, my friendly & sometimes unfriendly mind stream, *constantly creating both samsara & nirvana* - as Saraha has said. To those unfamiliar w. Buddhist vocabulary, please forgive my inability to *make it new* & suffer through the notes, written for you.

Living on Margarita Island, or in Bagnore, as I have been privileged to do, both places an extension of the indefinable *bodhicitta* or loving kindness - offered by Namkhai Norbu Rinpoche, to whom The Book L is dedicated, one takes notice first of all, of nature. One wonders why we ever departed fr. the deep harmonic, to align ourselves w. anything but the miracle that is daily & without effort presented to us.

I close w. a poem by Emily Dickinson, conferred upon me, by one of my night companions, as often, in NYC, where this manuscript was formalized, I was too tired to take the long ride 'home'.

    I've got an arrow here;
      Loving the hand that sent it,
    I the dart revere.

    Fell, they will say, in "skirmish"!
      Vanquished, my soul will know,
    By but a simple arrow
      Sped by an archer's bow.

Louise Landes Levi
New York City - 2009

www.ingramcontent.com/pod-product-compliance
Lightning Source LLC
Chambersburg PA
CBHW031125080526
44587CB00011B/1122